DEAR FATHER

A Collection of Essays and Letters

BY

Erick Ochieng Otieno • Vivienne Kapkarich

Sonia Mitchell • Alex Matiko • Nicholas Matthews

Collins Agesa • Lovender Mirenja • Cara Loto

Cynthia Mwakio • John Engenyule Twiza

Maya Bambina • Giuseppe Boy • Kegwa Bonita

Winfred Barbari • Teresa Yego • Bella Doozy

Fratello Gemello • Jombaa Onkel

Published by NOVELTY FICTION

www.novelty-fiction.com

Table of Contents

Protector by Vivienne Kapkarich...4

Preface...5

Acknowledgements..6

Dedication..9

Chapter 1 by Vivienne Kapkarich...11

Chapter 2 by Lovender Mirenja..15

Chapter 3 by Cara Loto...19

Chapter 4 by Erick Ochieng 21

Chapter 5 by Cynthia Mwakio...24

Chapter 6 by John Engenyule Twiza...30

Chapter 7 by Maya Bambina...44

Chapter 8 by Giuseppe Boy...50

Chapter 9 by Kegwa Bonita..52

Chapter 10 by Sonia Mitchell..55

Chapter 11 by Alex Matiko..58

Chapter 12 by Nicholas Matthews...61

Chapter 13 by Collins Agesa..64

Chapter 14 by Winfred Barbari...66

Chapter 15 by Teresa Yego..67

Chapter 16 by Bella Doozy...71

Chapter 17 by Fratello Gemello...76

Chapter 18 by Jombaa Onkel 79

About the Authors...102

PROTECTOR

by Vivienne Kapkarich

When I was falling,
You rose and caught me,
Protected me and lifted me,
Once again it was a priceless act,
A caring and loving protector.

You reminded me of patience,
The power of education and,
The unkind life out there,
With stubbornness, I saw it funny,
Still, you were a determined protector.

Most people gave up on me,
A father like you is all I need,
A black sheep I was named,
I was their laughingstock,
Lucky me, I had you for protection.

I remember the game boards,
They'll make you brighter, you said,
You taught me until I beat you to it,
I never knew your words would be my life guide,
You protected my life, with board game moves.

Our indifference never disintegrated us,
Your passing news left me devastated,
But knowing you for twenty-five years,
Has left me brighter and brighter,
Though gone, your words are yielding.

PREFACE

Everyone has a story to tell, and after reading the poem Protector from Eminent Desire, a collection of poems by Vivienne Kapkarich, an idea came to me. It reflects how the father figure has never been as appreciated or felt such closeness towards their children compared to their counterparts – namely, the mother figure.

I realized that I never got close to my father to the point of opening up about his failures or achievements. Then I thought: why not write a letter expressing all these feelings and emotions, addressing him, telling him all that I was afraid to say, whether good or bad?

On the same note, I thought: why not compile a book of letters from volunteering individuals who hold something inside that they would want to tell their fathers, whether deceased or living? I felt that such a project would be a good opportunity for people to finally get off their chest what they wanted to tell their father.

Fear of reprisals, uncertainty about how to express oneself, or a lack of opportunity may have caused someone to remain silent. At this time, eighteen authors will be letting go of what was never shared during any father-son or father-daughter moment.

– *Erick Ochieng Otieno*

ACKNOWLEDGMENTS

I would like to express my gratitude to the Almighty Jah for the wisdom and courage given to me to bring this idea into reality, without fear holding me back.

I want to express my gratitude to my co-collaborator, Ms. Vivienne Kapkarich, who is not only a fellow author and poet but also a dear friend and colleague. She put a tremendous amount of effort into developing this anthology. She embraced the project as her own, and successfully collected as many stories as possible to feature in this book.

I would like to express my gratitude to Mr. Morten Rand, our editor, and his publishing firm, Novelty Fiction, for accepting this idea when it was first pitched to him. We appreciate all the effort and time you put into making this book a success.

To all the volunteers who decided to participate in this project and my friends who supported me – Alex Matiko, Collins Aseto, Collins Agesa, and Joy Kamau; thank you for your solidarity, I do appreciate it.

- Erick Ochieng Otieno

The memory of my late father, Didymus Kiboi Siyoi, fondly remembered as Mwalimu (teacher), and of the experiences we shared, have been the cornerstone of my work on this book. It is equally important for me to recognize his siblings, who have upheld his legacy since his departure.

I have received tremendous support from many people in furthering my writing career, and am immensely grateful to them. Their efforts and support have been invaluable to me, and their advice has also been extremely beneficial during the creation of this book.

I wish to extend my heartfelt gratitude to the following individuals: Mrs. Ruth Napkawa Machenje, my dear aunt and friend; Mr. Erick Ochieng Otieno, my lifelong best friend, co-author, and poet, whose vision inspired this book; my best friend, Mr. Wycliffe Arende Oloo, alongside Ms. Tabitha Kamene Mutua, Mr. Haresh Gohil Rambai, and Ms. Roda Muthoka Mumbua; my cousin, Ms. Carolyne Kapkarich, for her fervent support of this project; my mentors, Ms. Sera Naiti Muiah and Ms. Trephonia Ngina Nzioka; and in loving memory of my late mother, Julia Simuli Machenje, whose presence in my thoughts has been a constant source of motivation to continue writing. My deepest appreciation goes out to each one of you.

The laborious tasks required for the empirical research needed to complete the book were graciously undertaken by a team including Mr. Brian Kipruto Siyoi, Ms. Mary Egwah, Ms. Lovender Mirenja, Mr. Joseck Shambi, Ms. Winfred Barbari Kimachas, Ms. Beauty Dzame Mkoba, Ms. Patriciah Sindinyu, Mr. George Masika Kubo, Ms. Cynthia Mwakio, Ms. Teresa Yego, and the Engenyule family. Their diligence and attention to detail were exceptional, and they approached their tasks as if they had a genuine stake in the project. I am incredibly grateful to them.

Finally, I want to recognize the numerous individuals who have contributed to our work with their honesty, openness, and willingness to share their stories. They have a powerful message for their fathers.

– *Vivienne Kapkarich*

DEDICATION

We dedicate this book to all the fathers around the globe, whether alive or deceased. These essays and letters are for you, and we hope you will feel much appreciated for your good deeds or forgive yourself for the negative experiences you had with your children.

To the children: by reading these essays and letters, we hope you will feel comfortable appreciating a father in your life, whether he is alive, deceased, or you have no clue who he is. Keep appreciating him for giving you life, and don't forget to value all father figures in general.

To everyone: we hope that by reading this story, you will gather the courage to show gratitude not only to yourself but also to the people around you. Such a gesture from you will surely make this world a better place.

- Erick Ochieng Otieno
- Vivienne Kapkarich

CHAPTER 1

by Vivienne Kapkarich

Dear Dad,

I hope you are resting peacefully wherever you are. Today marks the seventh anniversary of your passing. It's a day when I once again remember you through my writing, and I hope you will accept my letter with an open heart.

Growing up, I never realized the need for a protector until you became one. I am incredibly excited to proclaim that you are the bravest protector in my life. While most children grow up with the love of both parents simultaneously, I experienced this love separately, which has shaped me into a better person.

I remember that when we were young, you would often come to hand my brother and me some money. I recall you arriving at our playground while we played with other children, and we would have to dash over to you. You would evenly split the cash you held, and hand it to my brother and me to deliver to our mother If the cash couldn't be divided equally, my brother would receive the larger share. This used to upset me, but you would explain that he should get more, being the elder. The moment you said, "Take this to your mom," we would sprint to her in a fierce race and hand over the cash. Wow! Looking back I see the humor in it. I'm certain we never said thank you. We indeed were a handful.

The sudden death of my mother was as devastating for

you as it was for us. Nevertheless, her passing provided an opportunity for us to get to know each other. Initially, living with you was challenging; I was accustomed to having my mother around, and adjusting to a stepmother wasn't something I was prepared for. However, I am grateful that you helped us feel at ease in the new environment.

I want to express my gratitude for the numerous things you've done for me, which impacted me directly and indirectly. Having a strict father wasn't always enjoyable, but I've come to understand that those were life lessons. Now, I realize that nothing in life comes easily.

I recall the days when I was unfamiliar with checkers. You were persistent with us. Every Saturday morning, you'd wake us up to engage in a game after breakfast. You consistently won until we mastered the best strategies. When I began to win, I became your contender. We turned into checkers rivals, and our matches felt like derbies. Reflecting societal expectations that a girl should focus on household chores, many disapproved of our playing games. I'm not sure why this never troubled you, but I suspect that in your fatherly wisdom, you understood that I had to transcend societal norms.

The board game I stumbled upon, the one you taught me to use to outmaneuver my rivals, has shown me how to navigate the world. It's a game of life I didn't master until then. Checkers, among many things, has helped me broaden my thinking and improve myself over time, so that I can proudly announce that I have learned how to play the game of life.

Throughout my life I've faced challenging times when people abandoned me due to my stubbornness. Yet, I count myself lucky to have a father like you, who consistently had faith in me even when no one else did. You've been my pillar of support and my guardian. Even though I was labeled the black sheep and became the butt of many jokes, you never wavered in your belief in me. Your steadfast support has been the source of my strength, and for that I am eternally thankful.

The saying goes that parents know their children best. I didn't understand why you gave me this advice, but I bet it's because you knew me well. You said, "Work hard in school and secure a career that doesn't require much energy." To this day, I'm unsure why you told me this. Sometimes, I think it was because my health complications made you worry about my future. At other times, I believe it's just advice parents routinely give their children, since no one wants their child to struggle in life. After reading a series of Rich Dads books, I think I have a clue. I'm sincerely thankful for this advice.

Being your child has brought other father figures into my life. If I were to end this letter without acknowledging their contributions, it would constitute an act of ingratitude. Your siblings have significantly impacted my life, overseeing my professional education, ensuring my basic needs are met, and making sure I lack nothing. I am truly thankful to them. They embody the essence of fatherhood, and since your passing, they have filled your shoes at every milestone in my life. Many would not extend such support to their brother's children, which makes me hold you and them in high esteem.

I may not be certain of your pride in me, but I hope that my humble accomplishments in life will earn it. I am grateful for the vast knowledge I have gained from you, as I continue to grasp more of the lessons you've imparted.

To you, my father, and the father figures you have left behind, please accept this letter as a token of my gratitude. Thank you for being the foundation of who I have become.

Thankfully,
- *Your child*

CHAPTER 2

by Lovender Mirenja

I am deeply grateful to God for keeping my father alive long enough to witness my growth and journey through life. Having him by my side as a source of guidance, wisdom, and support has been a tremendous blessing. Reflecting on our relationship, I sometimes feel it would be appropriate to greet him with "Shikamo," a traditional Swahili gesture of respect for elders. Often used to show appreciation and reverence for the wisdom and experience that elders possess, the gesture is deeply rooted in African culture.

However, I'm not entirely certain if my father would understand the gesture or respond as intended. While society places a lot of emphasis on respecting our elders, I don't necessarily agree with it, and I believe that my father shares this view. Never being one to demand respect based on his age or status, he has always treated me as an equal. Therefore, greeting him in such a way might raise concerns and cause him confusion, which could lead to misunderstandings.

I don't want to cause any unnecessary tension or discomfort between us, especially given how crucial our relationship is to me. I believe that our bond is based on mutual trust, respect, and understanding, so that no formal gesture is necessary to express my appreciation of him. Rather, I will continue to treasure our moments together and strive to make him proud through my actions and accomplishments.

As a young child, I had a close relationship with my dad, and our bond grew even stronger over the years. One time, when I was around 10 years old, I pretended to be sick so that I could skip school. My dad quickly saw through my act but decided to spend time with me, anyway. He took me to his studio, where we spent hours painting and drawing. I was amazed by his artistic talent, and he patiently taught me new techniques and skills.

As we worked, my dad surprised me by creating a beautiful portrait of me. He added all sorts of details and illustrations that made me feel special and unique. It was a moment I'll never forget – I felt so loved and appreciated.

Despite my attempts to draw him looking like a scarecrow, my dad was always patient and never took offense. He encouraged me to keep drawing, and helped me improve my skills. With each visit to his studio, I learned something new and grew more confident in my abilities.

Looking back on those memories, I realize how lucky I was to have such a caring and supportive dad. Our time in the studio brought us closer together, and I cherish those moments to this day.

That was also where I had a life-changing experience, which made me appreciate him and enjoy his company even more. My dad played a character that taught me how a man can control his anger because he has power over it. I experienced this aspect of his personality in action, which had a positive impact on me. His portrayal of the character was so powerful that it influenced my life.

On a personal level, I have struggled to deal with men who exhibit traits such as disrespectful language, uncontrolled anger, violence, and toxicity. Because of my dad's demonstration, I knew that these behaviors can be controlled, except some men choose not to. My father set a perfect example for me, and I cannot recall us ever arguing or having any sort of disagreement.

Because of my dad's example, I believe that men generally have power over their emotions and are quite good at emotional intelligence. With my father as a role model, I believe that no man should be arrogant or violent towards me because I wouldn't tolerate it. I learned from the best, my father, whose guidance has helped me become more assertive and confident in my dealings with men.

My greatest desire is to celebrate this Father's Day alongside my dad, revisiting our cherished moments in the studio, dabbling in inks, crafting drawings, and creating award-worthy paintings. Its a time to immerse ourselves in the joy of art and forge new memories. I'm eager to see his reaction to the progress in my drawing abilities. I'm confident that I can now capture his likeness in a portrait, and it's something I'm looking forward to sharing with him.

Despite the separation from my mother, this man remains unparalleled. He embraced his paternal duties with unwavering commitment. I am convinced that my father set a standard of fatherhood that surpasses many who falter in their responsibilities despite having an unbroken family. He is my hero, and I yearn for the opportunity to express this to him directly – to embrace him, to declare my love for him, and to affirm that, in my eyes, he is the epitome of excellence.

Throughout my life journey, I've come to understand that no matter the distance, we should never hesitate to express our feelings to our loved ones. It's important to let them know how much we appreciate their presence in our lives. This is a lesson my father has taught me, and it's a message I intend to share with the world. We must stand united as a family, embracing our differences.

My dad is an exceptional person. He's warm-hearted, compassionate, and always puts his family first. He's also incredibly hardworking, and never gives up on anything he sets his mind to. No matter what challenges life throws his way, he always manages to overcome them with grace and determination.

But my dad isn't just a hard worker, he's also outgoing and fun to be around. He's always up for an adventure, whether it's trying a new restaurant, exploring a new city, or just spending time with his family and friends. I feel lucky to have such a well-rounded and dynamic person in my life.

Of course, my dad is only human. Like all of us, he's made mistakes along the way. But despite any missteps, I believe that God gave me the perfect dad. He's taught me so much about life and love, and I'm grateful for every moment that I get to spend with him.

In a world where any male can become a father, it takes a truly special person to be a dad. And I'm lucky enough to have one of the best.

CHAPTER 3

by Cara Loto

Dear Dad,

I'm kind of anxious about how you'll react to my greeting; I'm not sure what to expect.

You failed in the most fundamental aspect of being a father, which is to ensure the safety and well-being of your children. This crucial quality, ingrained in me since childhood, was noticeably absent in you.

Whenever I reflect on my life, I am overwhelmed by feelings of shame and disappointment. I often feel like my existence has brought disgrace to you and our family. It's as if my birth is viewed as something abhorrent. I struggle to express this, but I harbor deep feelings of resentment towards you, and sometimes wish I had never been born.

How could you do this to me at such a young age? You molested me, abused me, and even blackmailed me not to tell my mother. You went into a league with Mom, and married me off when I was very young. I became a mother when I should have been simply a child.

I have lived a miserable life. I used to believe that your way of living was the right one, so I followed in your footsteps, hurting everyone around me. I ran away from the marriage you forced me into. After leaving two of my children with their father, I even paid someone to have a child with me. I have lived a dishonest life, mistakenly thinking that it was the best way to live, and I have hurt people who were kind to me.

You are a criminal, and made me one as well. Today, I'm living a life that takes me in and out of courts, relying on the mercy of well-wishers. I thought that if you could get away with wrongdoing, so could I, but unlucky me got caught.

I never gained anything positive from our relationship. Now, I am putting in a lot of effort to better myself with the support of my friends. Reflecting on our past, I feel deep regret. I am a mother of three children, feeling uncertain about my future.

You were supposed to be my father, but saw me as a sex toy. I'm your blood, but you have bad blood. I detest you with passion. And for the said reason, you cannot be my dad. I refuse you in my life.

Finally, I don't believe I can stay with you in the same house, where I could easily do something harmful to you. I believe I have grown enough to tackle you. I hope you rot in the jail of your conscience.

I hope you will come to terms with who you are, and never do such things to any other child, whether in this life or the next.

I hope you repent.

  – Your child

CHAPTER 4

by Erick Ochieng

Dear Dad,

It's me, your beloved son. For many days, I have been wanting to express my feelings to you about certain things that have happened in our lives. However, due to the fear of facing your reaction concerning these sensitive issues, I have been holding back. Now, they feel like a ticking time bomb ready to explode any minute. I believe expressing them in writing will ease the burden off my chest and help me overcome my fear by letting you know.

You've been a great father to my siblings and me. As a child, I saw you doing your best to provide for us, but I only realized everything that was happening behind the scenes when I grew up.

I have learned a lot from you, and the great lessons of life came from your way of life. I've come to understand the disadvantages of debts, being too generous, polygamy, and conditional love – that's how you led your entire life.

I also know the advantages of living together as one family and in love. I have learned how to welcome and accept strangers, because of how you used to interact and live with them.

Dad, I always remember when you used to drive us to Mombasa city during weekends, and it was an awesome adventure. The gifts you used to get me when I performed well in school made some of the best days of my life. Like when you got me my second bicycle, a BMX, I was really overwhelmed. I also remember when you helped me with a job search, and managed to secure a position for me with a local contractor.

Whenever I listen to Musa Juma's song "Ratego Baba," memories of you flood my mind. I get to think about you a lot, and wish more life on you. Your whole life revolved around cars, so I would like to celebrate you with a special gift: your favorite car.

I would like to understand what happened in your life. You used to be wealthy, but it seems that you didn't follow some instructions and forgot to seek guidance, which led to your downfall.

If only you had been open to listening and seeking guidance, perhaps your life wouldn't have taken that difficult turn.

You are a good man full of ideas. I guess I take after you in that regard. What surprises me is that all the ideas you implemented were good but failed terribly. What could have been the problem? Was it poor planning or lack of information?

I pray to God every day to remember you in your endeavors and to remind you of your purpose. The reports I receive are discouraging and shameful, and I don't want to believe a single word of what I hear.

You're still my father, and I will remain to be your son no matter what, come rain or sunshine. I still do remember your advice and what you require me to do as your son. That's a mandate I will fulfill, you don't have to worry.

I know we have had our differences from time to time, but I'm glad we got to sort them out, then move on. I love you, and am proud of you for the efforts you did for us – at least, you did try.

For now, I have eased the burden of these emotions within me. I hope that one day, this letter will find its way to you. If not, maybe in the next life I shall have the courage to tell you all this, so we can share one-on-one. But that's it for now.

– Your loving son

CHAPTER 5

by Cynthia Mwakio

Growing up with a father figure like you was a roller coaster ride -- an amazing and sometimes terrifying experience at home.

I would never say you were a bad father, absolutely not.

You have always been the best dad, a wonderful father, and a devoted husband to Mom. Never in my life have I heard you argue with her. Nor has she ever raised her voice because you berated or scolded her. All she does is shower you with praise and speak positively of you.

Growing up with a military dad was an experience of extremes, a roller coaster of both spoken and unspoken events, the missed moments, the joy, the seriousness and diligence you instilled in us, the multitude of morals and beliefs you embedded within us, the proper conduct we were to display whether you were present or not, the laughter and jokes you shared, and the many lonely nights spent in your absence. We often felt the void of your absence during our tender years, when we needed you most. Throughout those delicate and innocent times, your presence was intermittent. I value your dedication and understand that your demanding job required your focus.

When I was young, I might not have been fully aware of your absence, but no child overlooks the absence of a family member. Your absence cast a shadow over us. It is commonly understood that the father is the provider of security and the protector of the family. In our situation, a crucial member of our family was frequently missing.

I recall the days long past; surely, Mama had many sleepless nights. I'm certain she held onto you in the many moments she missed you and wished you were near. In the numerous letters she penned, she must have poured out heartfelt emotions. You know the rest, Papa.

As you were always traveling around the world, we missed you to such an extent that we formed a strong bond with Mom. We couldn't grasp your frequent presence and absence. I hope you understand why we became more attached to her. She was always there with us, to the point where we would run and hide at the sight of you. It wasn't that we didn't love you, no. You appeared to us as a whole new, yet familiar package, but one that was rarely in our view – as the saying goes, "Out of sight, out of mind." I hope you won't blame us for everything. Now that we've grown, we've come to better understand why you were only present occasionally. Your presence still resonates with us, your attributes and character always manifest at home, whether consciously or subconsciously.

How you brought us up has shaped my personality. Everyone can attest to the lifestyle we were accustomed to, especially those with a parent in the military can relate to these experiences.

Every military family receives constant protection, which I greatly appreciated and enjoyed. I admired the times we were escorted to school by soldiers, and similarly when returning home.

I recall an incident when, as usual, we were dropped off by military vehicles. That evening, the same vehicle was supposed to pick us up from school. On this particular day, my elder sister and I stood across from the school gate, awaiting our ride. The soldiers arrived, collected my sister, and inadvertently left me behind. I stood there emotionless, not waving, crying, or making any move.

Reflecting on that precise moment, I reassure myself that I was indeed born to make a move. In those fleeting seconds, I realized that my strong personality has been with me since childhood – challenging and resilient. During that instance, fear was absent, panic a stranger, and worry about the vehicle's return the least of my concerns. I was prepared for any outcome, simply watching the vehicle as it disappeared into the distance.

Fortunately, the vehicle returned to fetch me. I'm led to believe that my sister pleaded with the soldiers. I firmly believe it was your personality, the robust character you passed on to us, that we all embody. I am convinced that fearlessness is indeed within us. I now realize that the upbringing found in military life is not for the faint-hearted. Such memories reflect the brave character we have inherited from you.

Dad, you're the best. I congratulate you for the countless times you went out there to fight for your nation and for us, ensuring a better and more fulfilling life. You've met all of our needs and continue doing so. Your hard work is a generational attribute that I've witnessed in my grandparents, in you, and in every one of your siblings, and it has been passed down to us I still see the zeal you possess. It is unmatched. As you often say, "Once a soldier, always a soldier."

Your love for us was, and remains, profound. I hold dear the memories of the many gifts you brought back from the different countries you visited. Occasionally, I find myself wishing to turn back time to relive those moments. Truly, childhood was a delight.

Whenever we saw you, our eyes would lighten up, though we feared your presence because you never entertained silly plays. We expected to be punished. You loved whipping us with a special whip only the military possessed, mostly used by Asus. We were always scared to go wrong, knowing that no misdeed would go unpunished.

Whenever you were around, we experienced a sense of security and protection, yet your strict personality and seriousness also intimidated us. As part of the team that safeguarded the nation, your presence at home meant we had the utmost security. Fear was not something we felt, our only apprehension stemming from your stern persona and upright demeanor.

The memories I've shared are meant to demonstrate and convey my deep gratitude and appreciation for you, and to emphasize the significance of your presence in our lives.

There's an unforgettable instance that occasionally creeps into my mind, one that I've always found it difficult to comprehend. It's a story Mom told us.

One night, our home was encircled by a band of thieves. Hearing noises outside, Mom swiftly ascended to the balcony for a clearer view. With her pregnancy advanced, my anxiety surged upon learning of the situation, especially with you not being home. I can scarcely fathom the turmoil Mom endured in those moments; undoubtedly, she thought of you, not for protection against the forty assailants, but for the solace your presence brings. The terror she must have experienced could nearly have triggered premature labor.

That night, my mum and aunty were with us. Her screams in the bedroom woke the entire neighborhood. Yet, surprisingly, the thieves who had entered our house did not hear the screams, nor did they catch a glimpse of our hiding spot.

These groups had a notorious gang name, and were infamous for wreaking havoc on the wealthiest individuals in the area. Back then, we lived in Nyali, Mombasa. On the day they planned to strike, knowing my father was away, my mother went to the top balcony. There, she spoke with a neighbor about sounding the alarm. The neighbor did not disappoint; she alerted everyone, and the neighborhood became vigilant. Realizing their peril, the thieves abandoned their machetes and blunt instruments, then vanished. The next day, two soldiers were stationed in our compound until you returned.

Father, you're the best dad; we cherish your presence and want to express how vital it is to us.

Your persistent hard work, perseverance, humor, intellect, creative innovation, essential nature, and – notably – your robust physique are always cherished and admired.

I love you, Dad.

CHAPTER 6

by John Engenyule Twiza

I would greet my father with "hujambo." This is a respectful greeting in our culture. In return, for the short time I knew my father, he liked being official and would greet me by saying "hujambo."

When I was a toddler, 3 years old or younger, my father used to come home from work regularly. However, when I was about 4 or 5, my parents started having domestic issues that seemingly went unresolved, making things complicated. My dad worked as a carpenter; and sometimes, when he arrived home and my mom asked about food, he would respond angrily. Sometimes, my mom would just leave to get some fresh air. One day, the issues escalated into a terrible fight that drew the attention of our neighbors. After this incident, my mom decided to leave with my two young siblings, and they wound up staying at her friend's place. My dad and I remained home, but we were scared of what might happen next as our household had never experienced such fights before.

My father continued to go to work, and my mom used to come and check on me during the day. Eventually, they resolved their issues, so that my mother and siblings came back home to stay with us. Things returned to normal, and we were okay.

One day, a fight broke out again, but this time my

mother stood firm. She refused to leave, knowing clearly that her home with her family was where she belonged. She adamantly told our dad that he should be the one to leave. My dad gave in and said, "It's okay." The next day, Father told Mom to prepare breakfast for him and pack his bag. As a carpenter, he worked far away for days or weeks at a time once he had secured a contract. This was routine and nothing suspicious to us. We knew he was going to work. He carried his favorite multipurpose brown bag packed with his clothes and tools.

My father wasn't a friendly person. When he got home, we would keep ourselves busy to stay away from him. All he did was give us orders of what to do and how to answer. So when he left, we watched him go without saying goodbye. We were uncomfortable around him, so his absence felt like a relief. We hoped he would be gone for a month or so, and we would have less tension in the house. Little did we know that this would be the last day for us to see our father. I was six years old at the time, and have a vivid memory of it.

Dad left, and days went by. We heard that he was in Kitale, our hometown. After months, we heard that he had moved on. We were concerned since this wasn't his normal routine. Normally, he would have come back home before proceeding to other towns for new tasks. We wondered if he was even coming back. At that time, as kids, we had no sense of the calendar; we marked years with Christmas celebrations. Once Christmas had been celebrated, we knew that the year was over. We celebrated the first Christmas, but Dad was nowhere to be seen. We wondered why he wasn't coming back. Mom tried asking around for his whereabouts, and was informed that he had moved to Nakuru, which is the city nearest to Eldoret, around a two-and-a-half hours drive. We hoped he would come, knowing he had finished his work in Eldoret and was to start a new task in Nakuru. We celebrated the 2nd Christmas, and got even more worried. When Mom asked around, she found out that he had moved to Nairobi, the capital of Kenya. He was currently working there.

Life became tough for us after our father, the breadwinner, left. We were living in a rented house, and for two years we owed money to the landlord. He grew impatient with us and started threatening to evict us. It was understandable; he was just protecting his property. Our situation looked bleak as my father had made the decision to leave us, and we were left alone with my mother. We celebrated our third Christmas with little hope. Years went by, and we heard nothing from him. Back then, there were no telephones available for communication, and sending letters took ages. It was a tough time for us in terms of staying in touch.

In our hometown, if someone was away from home for a long time, people would sometimes assume that a family member had passed away, and a telegram would be sent to encourage that person to come back home. My mother tried this approach, but in vain. She was relying on the kindness of others and struggling with debt. Our situation worsened, and we were eventually evicted.

During this difficult period, my second-eldest sister had gone to visit our maternal grandmother, then gotten married.

Our eldest brother decided to follow our father's trend of moving from Kitale to Eldoret, then from Eldoret to Nakuru, and finally from Nakuru to Nairobi. Meanwhile, our dad had extended his travels to Mombasa, and our eldest brother joined him there.

Our third-oldest brother decided to start working at a young age, going around the town washing dishes in hotels to at least secure some food for us. The rest of us, including my elder brother, two young sisters, and younger brother, were too little and had no idea about how to improve upon our situation. We wandered around with our mom trying to survive, often begging in the streets.

After three days of sleeping out in the cold, my mom and our neighbors were all wondering how we would be saved. Asked where she thought she could get help, my mom thought that only her parents' home could help us. Our neighbors raised funds for the five of us to travel from Kitale to Kakamega. We boarded the Matatu at 3 AM, and the driver agreed to pick us up with our luggage first before letting on other passengers. We didn't have enough money to carry all our luggage, so we had to make do with just the essentials. Our mother secured a seat, while the rest of us had to stand from youngest to eldest.

We arrived in Kakamega, ready to start a new chapter of our lives. My grandparents welcomed us warmly, but it wasn't long before family politics emerged. There was sibling rivalry, and my uncles were adamant that my mother shouldn't return home. According to societal norms, a married woman, especially when dowry has been paid, should not leave her matrimonial home. Therefore, my mother had brought shame upon the family. Fortunately, some uncles supported our stay there. We witnessed intense drama between siblings, and a decision had to be made. Ultimately, my mother chose to stay with her parents, while we were supposed to return to our father or his relatives.

My aunt, who is our father's sister, lived in Kakamega. Since she was directly related to him, she was supposed to take us in on behalf of our father's brother. Her place was about an hour's walk from my mother's hometown. We were not familiar with the area, so we had to ask around for directions. We didn't leave on the same day; instead, we stayed at our granny's for a few days, but each day was filled with new drama. We were the topic of every conversation. My uncles would come back from drinking, and the same arguments would start over again. We had no other option but to listen to all the nasty things being said.

One morning, my mother thought of our elder sister, who lived nearby, and decided she'd take us to stay with our aunt. After being informed by a local during market day, my sister arrived. Information was commonly exchanged on market days, as people from various villages gathered to sell and buy goods. Although it took several days, the message reached her. At that time, one of my cousins from Nairobi was visiting and in need of house help. My sister, despite her youth, went to assist with the household chores. She then left for Nairobi. This left three of us at home: my elder brother, my younger brother, and myself. Eventually, our sister arranged for us to join our aunt.

Our aunt welcomed us warmly; but later, we accidentally overheard her complaining to her daughter about the burden my father had left on her – us. We had no other means of survival. The domestic strife between my parents stemmed from this issue. My mother had a sensible idea that my father refused to consider. To her, it was illogical to rent a house when my father owned land where we could build our own home and save on rent. This disagreement was the root of their conflict. Ultimately, my father secretly sold the land and squandered the money. My mother's suggestion to invest in a new place only fueled his anger. He left us destitute, unaffected by our suffering. My aunt bluntly stated that our father had selfishly consumed all the proceeds from the land sale, and that we were now imposing on others instead of seeking him out. We were his responsibility, she insisted, no one else's. Despite knowing we were unwelcome, we stayed. Life was difficult.

Eventually, my aunt reached her limit. Her daughter was her main source of support, so she declared that she wouldn't be providing for three extra people. She made it clear that to continue receiving financial help, she would have to let us go. My cousin suggested that her mother should allow us to stay with our uncle, my father's brother. She agreed to provide transportation for us to go to his place. Our elder sister was called upon once more to escort us to Soi, where my uncle resides. Carrying our luggage, we boarded the bus in town. However, the money we had for transport ran out before we reached our destination. At one junction, our attempts to hitch a ride were futile. My sister decided we should take any vehicle going in our direction. We caught a bus, and when the conductor came for the fare, my sister promised to pay upon disembarking, as she couldn't access her purse at that moment. Upon arrival, when the conductor demanded payment, my sister admitted she had no money. An argument ensued, but other passengers, weary from their journey, felt the conductor was delaying them and urged him to let us go. My sister's shrewdness saved us that day, and we finally reached Soi.

We traversed the marram road, inquiring for my uncle's residence, as its exact location was unknown to us. After an extensive walk, hunger, thirst, and fatigue had set in. It felt like an eternity before we finally reached my uncle's place. There, we found him and his wife seated around a fire. Upon us entering the compound, they welcomed us warmly. My uncle inquired about our visit, and my sister relayed that our aunt had sent us to stay with him since our mother had returned to her childhood home. Hearing this, my uncle, in a fit of anger, hurled the stool he was sitting on towards my sister, exclaiming, "Was I present when your father sold the land that you come to encamp here?" Fortunately, my sister evaded the stool. She then stood and requested to use the bathroom to freshen up before continuing their conversation. However, she did not return, and we were left clueless about her journey back to Kakamega.

My uncle was upset with us; our presence seemed to remind him of our father's mischievous ways. We felt like refugees in his home. Our grandmother, who lived with him, was elderly and blind. Yet, her blindness didn't stop her from noticing us. When she heard noises, she inquired if we were her grandchildren, recognizing our voices. She invited us to stay with her in her modest abode, a single-roomed house with a grass-thatched roof. Interestingly, she could identify everything within her home. Initially, I suspected she was feigning blindness, as I had never encountered someone like her.

My grandmother was served dinner by my uncle as usual, while we were left hungry. Granny kindly divided her meal into three portions, so that each of us could have a bite. It made us feel better. Despite her failing eyesight, she was a compassionate woman. I am indebted to her for the care she showed us. After supper, we all shared one mattress, yet we were comfortable and content. Having little to smile about, any small kindness brought us joy. The following morning, we accompanied Granny to the farm to collect some extra leaves, which sustained us for the next few weeks until a neighbor intervened.

One of our uncles, who was married to one of my late aunts, took us in. He had been living alone since my aunt passed away. He lived close to my other uncle. He welcomed us into his overgrown house and told us that as men, we had to learn to survive. He was a kind-hearted man, who also struggled with alcohol. He showed us how to hustle and find something to eat. We started by collecting firewood and selling it to hotels in exchange for meals. It was difficult at first, but we eventually got used to it and found happiness in our new routine.

After looking for work, we found jobs at two different

homes. Both of the women who hired us had cows and needed help taking care of them. My brother was hired to take care of the cattle for a woman who owned many bovines, while I was responsible for caring for two cows for another woman. They welcomed us into their homes. During the day, my brother and I would herd the cattle, and in the evening, we would return to our respective bosses. These kind Christian women sheltered us, and we would eat together with their families. We had a lot to be thankful for.

One day, our mother and youngest brother came to visit us. Her health was deteriorating, and since they were staying far from us, we hoped our employers could help us by taking her in. They heard our request and took the issue to the church members. In fact, there was a house around the church that no one was living in. They suggested that my mum could live there and take care of the church. This offer was accepted, and my mom and brother had a roof over their heads. Our salary, which was very low at the time, went towards caring for them and ourselves. We never received monetary payment, but were given healthy meals, new clothes, and any medical attention needed. This sufficed for us.

At some point, my mother wanted to visit her distant brother, and she asked me to accompany her. We didn't know exactly where he lived, but it was only a few kilometers away. As we walked together towards his place, the journey was tiring, especially for my mum. She seemed unwell, but insisted that I walk ahead of her. I would walk for a bit and then wait for her before continuing. That day is very significant to me, and I often find myself contemplating it.

I sat down and waited for her to reach me. She stood up, looked at me, and said, "My son, at this point, there is nothing more I can do. I'm leaving you in the hands of God because there is no one else I can leave you with." We embarked on the remainder of our journey. After a few minutes, she picked up a piece of sugarcane lying on the ground, and gave it to me to eat. "Eat, my son. People can deny you food, but God can't. Eat the sugarcane, for I, your mother, have given it to you." Finally, we arrived at our destination. We were warmly welcomed, and stayed there for two days.

My mother was still feeling unwell, and thus we journeyed to one of her relatives' place. We informed the man of her situation and hoped for a better way forward. The two agreed that Mum should go back home to her parents, since traditional herbs would be the most suitable treatment for her.

My mother and little brother went back home, leaving behind my elder brother and me. We were used to seeing our mother every day, and life was a bit easier with her around. After she left, we felt a void in our hearts. Amidst this, my elder brother escaped from where he was working and went back to Kitale. I was taken in to replace him, taking care of the cattle. Months later, he returned and was hired to work at a different farm. Life kept moving on as we struggled to survive this stage of our childhood.

A few months passed, and we were informed that our elder sister had arrived. Whenever she was around, it meant either that we were being taken somewhere else or that something was wrong. I thought about this quietly. It was June of 1998. She had something to tell my brother and I. We had to go to the house of our uncle, who had previously chased us away. I wondered what could be so important that my sister had to return to a home where she was nearly hit by a chair and had to run away in the dark. Something wasn't adding up. She told us our mother had summoned us, so we packed our belongings and headed back to Kakamega.

While walking toward my grandparents' home in the dark evening, my sister informed us that even though we were heading to see our mother, she wasn't there. When we asked why, my sister simply said, "Mom is not there," and seemingly struggled to utter those words. We continued walking, my sister staying behind, and as we approached the compound, we heard her crying loudly. We, being kids, were unable to understand the reason, as our instincts hadn't matured sufficiently to grasp the situation. I was trying to figure things out, hoping to find everything okay.

Our aunts came to hug us, and that was when reality hit: our mother was no longer among us. It was painful to learn that she had already been buried. They took us behind the house to see her grave. In our culture, a married woman with children and paid dowry has no claim to her father's land. Since our mother was in this situation, they couldn't bury her traditionally. She had been buried behind my granny's house in the middle of the night. This chain of events has been a source of pain for me to this day. My dad owned land where my mom could have been buried with respect, but his actions made her an outcast of the family. It took me a long time to come to terms with the fact that she was gone. Not having seen her body, it all seemed unbelievable, like a work of fiction. Our younger brother had been the only witness to our mother's passing.

Things changed for us at that point. Our uncles recognized us as part of the family, and decided that my older brother should return to take care of the cattle. My younger brother and I went to live with our aunt, who also took me to school with my cousins. This was the first time I attended school. Meanwhile, my third older brother, who stayed in Kitale, had already gotten married and found a home for himself and his family. My younger brother was struggling with psychological trauma, likely caused by witnessing our mother's suffering. It was decided that my older brother would take him in and look after him, as he was able to, being somewhat established.

After two years, I joined my younger brother in Kitale and continued with my education. My brother took on the role of our father, and took care of me until I completed primary education. One day, I was sitting with my sister-in-law discussing what we should have for dinner. It was New Year's Eve, which was considered quite superstitious. Unintentionally, I used 200 Kenyan shillings to light up charcoal. As we were joking about the matter, my sister-in-law looked at the door and seemed shocked.

A man was standing by the door, holding a familiar-looking bag. My in-law had only seen my father in pictures, but she immediately recognized him and called me to welcome him. It was my father returning. Unsure of what to do since the homeowner was away, we all sat silent, looking at each other. My other brothers had come to celebrate the new year with us. Our host arrived, happy that he could celebrate with us for the first time in years instead of working. He noticed that there were more of us than when he left, took a closer look, and recognized our dad. He experienced mixed feelings and joined the silence. The joyful atmosphere of the house had come to a standstill.

Our cheerful relative broke the silence by serving food for my dad, which encouraged us to start talking. My father stayed at our neighbor's house because my brother's home was already crowded and couldn't accommodate him. After two days, we returned to our normal routine with him. Surprisingly, there was no tension as most of us had anticipated. He explained himself, and we all just nodded. We couldn't chase him away; after all, he was still our father. He attributed his mischievous behavior to Satan, as we usually do. We accepted what happened, and decided to move on with him.

After my brother took our father in, we tried to continue living as if nothing had happened. However, our father's health kept deteriorating until he eventually passed away due to illness. He was buried in my brother's compound. It seems like karma never spared my father for his past actions.

Writing a letter to my dad seemed tricky to me without explaining the ordeal we went through because of his negligence. Keeping this in mind will hopefully make my letter more understandable, and here it is:

Dear Father,

I hope you're resting well wherever you are. My family and I are doing well.

I'm not sure if you realize the impact your decisions had on us. I don't know if you are aware of the hardships we endured or the shame my mother suffered because of your choices.

Despite all this, you may be surprised to learn that given the chance to choose a father, I would still choose you. The challenges I faced in life have shaped the person I am today. I don't think I would be as hard-working, had I had a smoother life. Your decisions have influenced who I am, and I would still choose you for that reason. We are not perfect, and I have learned to lighten my burden by forgiving and appreciating people who own up to their mistakes.

In conclusion, I am grateful for the final words you shared with me on your deathbed. They have enriched me and provided moral support throughout my life. Your words, "You can take good care of the family," are the only gift I have ever received from you, and I cherish it deeply.

Father, you made our lives difficult. Unlike other kids, we never learned compassion when we were young. We became misfits in society. There is still damage within us, but all in all, I forgive you and wish that if you were given another life, you would become a better person than you were in this one.

Keep resting in peace.

– *Your son*

CHAPTER 7

by Maya Bambina

Growing up, I resided with my grandmother after my parents separated. My father worked in Mombasa, while my mother remained in our countryside home. According to my grandmother and other relatives, frequent arguments between my parents eventually culminated in their divorce.

My mother was compelled to return to her home, while my father stayed with us. This period was a difficult time in our lives, filled with complexities and issues. Amidst these challenges, we were obligated to go to court to decide which of our parents we preferred to live with.

My parents have four children: two daughters and two sons. In court, I decided to live with my father, while my sister chose to be with our mother. The youngest two siblings, being too little to make a choice, also went with our mother. Consequently, three of my siblings lived with our mother at our maternal grandmother's house, whereas I lived with my aunt in Mombasa. Despite the separation, our father ensured that all of us were well taken care of and wanted for nothing.

After my father remarried, he made the decision that I should relocate to live live with him, my stepmother and her son. During this time, my father displayed intense emotions that were difficult for us to comprehend. It led us to believe that there were underlying issues within the new family dynamic.

Living with my stepmom and stepbrother brought joy to

our home. Even though my mother and three siblings were not with us, I felt a sense of completeness. As a child, the complexities of life eluded me, but the happiness I experienced was undeniable and filled my days with contentment.

As time went by, my father decided to unite all his children under one roof. My three siblings came to live with us in Mombasa. Our family expanded from just us two children to five, including my three siblings and our stepbrother. My father had made what seemed like a logical decision, considering that my mother had already given up custody over my three siblings. I view what he did as a testament to his paternal responsibility. However, not everyone saw it as positive news. Some disapproved while others applauded this decision.

My stepmother was particularly upset. She constantly frowned upon the four of us, which was understandable from her perspective. The transition from raising two children to five must have been daunting. She received some misguided advice from her friends and family, which only compounded our difficulties. It was something we couldn't grasp at our age. Undoubtedly, we added to her burden, escalating her workload. Her demeanor turned toxic, moody, and angry, and from the way she treated us, it was clear we were the cause.

My father's behavior turned toxic as well. He began to physically abuse us without restraint. His actions were unrecognizable. I recall an incident when he brutally punished my brother for achieving 98% on a test instead of a perfect score. The mere fact that my brother missed a question on the test (to name a fruit with one seed, and he answered 'pawpaw') sent my father into a rage. As his pettiness and irresponsibility grew, he looked for the slightest reason to shout and beat us. Our lives turned into a living nightmare, one orchestrated by my father.

His behavior escalated to such a degree that the headteacher called him to the school for a stern warning about the physical abuse. Our teachers, alarmed by the recurring bruises that marred our health, had raised the alarm. Yet, this intervention did nothing to temper his actions; in fact, the violence worsened, leaving us battered and in fear for our lives. In desperation, my sister and I fled to the sanctuary of the local police station one night, too terrified to return home. We remained there, under the protection of the authorities, for two days, our dread of our father's wrath now a matter of police involvement.

On the third day, we attended school, and my paternal grandmother arrived. With her assistance, we returned home. This decision did not seem to please my stepmother, who apparently wanted us out of the house. I can only speculate that she may somehow have influenced my father to punish us so severely that we would run away and never return. She was relentless; it turned out that she had a significant thing in store for us.

Since we attended a nearby school, we would often come home during the lunch break, then head back for more classes. One day, her service was unlike any other time. Usually, following the main course, we would have a glass of soda or fresh juice. She had indeed prepared juice for us. She handed her son a glass of juice and instructed us to help ourselves, which was unusual, then left to run an errand. We thought we knew why she was being so moody: she had a misunderstanding with our dad the previous day.

My younger brother was a fast eater, and he finished his food well ahead of us. Then he proceeded to pour himself a glass of juice, as the rest of us kept on eating. After a few gulps of the juice, my brother started complaining of stomachache and fell down. His hands were on his stomach, and he was groaning with pain.

We were only kids and didn't know how to handle the situation, but my elder sister immediately phoned our dad, pleading with him to come home. My father rushed home on a motorbike, which he also used to bring my brother to the hospital.

Tests revealed that my brother suffered from food poisoning. Fortunately, he received timely medical attention, and once he felt better, my father called our stepmother and summoned her to come home As she did so, my father angrily instructed her to pack her things and leave. No doubt, our stepmother had intended to harm us; if we had all drunk the juice, it could have been fatal.

The poisoning incident served as a stark wake-up call for my father. Upon realizing the malevolent motives of our stepmother, he made the decisive move to separate from her that very day. He also called my grandma, asking her to come and take care of us. Since it would take her a day to travel to Mombasa, our nearby aunt came to pick us up. We stayed at her place for two days. My grandmother then came and stayed with us until the school semester was done, at which point we accompanied her to our father's hometown. We transferred schools and stayed with her for some time, visiting our father in Mombasa during holidays to spend time with him.

Returning to his true self, he embraced the role of a single father to four children. During this challenging period, my grandmother provided invaluable support and comfort. As I concluded my primary education and prepared for secondary school, my sister and I resided with our grandmother, while our brothers lived with our father. Our family maintained a close bond, with regular visits during holiday periods, which brought joy and fun into our lives.

Succeeding our mother and stepmom, my dad raised us without any complaints. He embraced his role as a father, and ensuring our success became his top priority. He always put us first, above all else. He had learned from his mistakes, albeit the hard way, but it was never too late for him. We grew to be proud of him. Through events involving my stepmom, we understood that he cherished us and would not let anyone harm us. I completed my secondary education and went on to college to pursue my professional education, with my dad making every impossibility possible for me.

I'm still on my journey to complete my college education, but am confident that I'll graduate soon and make my dad proud. Reflecting on my life, I see his presence in every step I've taken. Together, we've weathered the toughest times. Through these shared experiences, we've forged a deep and enduring bond.

I would certainly express my gratitude to him for his unwavering support. He has nurtured us with care and set a commendable example. Through his errors and guidance, he taught us valuable lessons and consistently advised us to be well-behaved children. He demonstrated the true meaning of discipline and steered us right whenever we strayed.

CHAPTER 8

by Giuseppe Boy

During my formative years, I had a father who was physically present, but emotionally and mentally absent. It was during those crucial periods when I needed his guidance and support the most that he was nowhere to be found. As a result, my development and education suffered greatly, and I was left to navigate the challenges of growing up on my own.

He would come home inebriated during the holidays, always appearing calm, but I was not open to him; my issues were always addressed with Mum.

During a specific phase of his life, he decided to tie the knot once again and moved to a new place, which caused us to lose contact for long periods of time, ranging from a few months to even years. As a result, I never had the opportunity to reconnect with him or share time together. It's a pity that our relationship has suffered from a lack of communication, and I hope to catch up with him at some point in the future.

On a certain day, I was at school when my father was summoned to the principal's office. It had been discovered that my school fees had not been paid, and I was told to go home. I immediately informed my father, hoping he would sort it out. Later that day, he came to pick me up, but I had no idea where we were going. He drove me to a bar and ordered a beer for himself. When I refused to drink, he gave me an ultimatum – either drink or walk back home alone. I asked him for fare money, but he bluntly refused, leaving me with no option but to walk back home, a distance of 7km. Making matters worse, my school fees remained unpaid, and the situation weighed heavily on me. This experience completely changed my relationship with my father.

In light of the ongoing difficulties we are facing, it can be challenging to find positive news to share. However, amidst all the chaos and uncertainty, one thing comes to my mind: the simple, yet thoughtful gesture of handing me a t-shirt as a gift during the holiday season. There is something truly special about wearing a brand-new shirt, with its soft and comfortable fabric, that can instantly uplift one's mood. The warmth and coziness of a new shirt can be particularly comforting in these difficult times when we are all trying to find ways to stay positive and keep our spirits high. A small but meaningful gesture of kindness can go a long way in bringing a smile to someone's face and spreading a little bit of joy and happiness.

CHAPTER 9

by Kegwa Bonita

In my family, it's customary for me to greet my father by saying: "Hi Dad." Without fail, he responds uniquely by saying: "Hi Mommy, are you fine?" It's a personalized and special way we have always greeted each other, one that makes me feel loved and appreciated.

I have a vivid memory of the day when I had to undergo sinus surgery. It was a nerve-wracking experience, but I was fortunate enough to have someone by my side who showed immense care and support. He stayed with me throughout the day, never leaving my side until I was discharged from the hospital. His presence and reassuring words helped ease my anxiousness and made the entire ordeal bearable.

On the night before Christmas, he would take us out to shop and make a merry family. We strolled through the bustling streets, admiring the bright lights and festive decor. We spent this time together browsing through the stores, picking out gifts for one another, and trying on clothes. We stopped to dine at a cozy restaurant, enjoying each other's company as we shared stories and laughter. There was no rush returning home, and we cherished every moment.

During my school days, he used to visit me quite frequently and generously hand me pocket money. His kind gestures made me feel appreciated and cared for during my formative years.

As a child, I fondly remember the times when my father and I would share jokes and laughter. Despite being a typical African dad with a no-nonsense approach to life, he always made time for us. However, there were times when we had to go through my mum to ask him for something because he considered certain things superfluous.

My father was known for his unwavering commitment to fairness. He always treated everyone with respect and kindness, regardless of their background, status, or beliefs. He believed that every person deserves to be treated justly and equally, and lived his life accordingly. His sense of fairness was not limited to his personal interactions, but extended to his professional and social life. Many people looked up to him, considering him a role model because of his sense of justice and equity.

Despite his ongoing struggles with alcoholism, my father was a responsible and devoted family man, and this weakness never stopped him from fulfilling his responsibilities towards us. Every year, he made it a priority to pay the school fees for my four siblings and I, no matter how difficult his financial situation. Despite his addiction, he always made sure that our basic needs were met, and our kitchen was stocked with enough food to feed our family of six month after month. It was no small feat, all things considered. In my eyes, he was the best father in the world, and given the chance, I would choose him again and again.

Words fail me as I try to articulate my feelings. My father was never one to be particularly expressive. Sadly, I never had the chance to reveal my true emotions towards him. If he were here today, he would be taken aback by the depth of my sentiments.

CHAPTER 10

by Sonia Mitchell

Dear Dad,

It's a good thing you're still alive, thank God for that, but I'm still disappointed in you. If by chance we got to meet, I know you would be confused once I greeted you with a handshake. Most likely, you would expect a warm, welcoming hug from your only daughter. I'm so sorry, but that will not happen because of my feeling that the handshake is enough and suitable for you.

I still remember the good moments we shared, like when you had a gift for me, a pair of new shoes just out of the blue, and I was amazed because I wasn't expecting anything. There was that other time when you gave me two hundred Kenyan shillings while under the influence of alcohol.

The most precious memory of all concerns the games we used to play together. I miss the pillow fights during our father-daughter time, the hide-and-seek games as well. We used to have fun with these activities, but unfortunately such good moments were exceptional.

Your anger issues really used to scare me. One particular time when I was in class four, I was so afraid to share my report card with you, the reason being that I had failed in your favorite subject, mathematics. I had to lie to avoid further confrontation, but eventually you found out and gave me the worst punishment of my life. Indeed, ignorance is bliss.

I'd wish I had simply given you the results to see for yourself instead of lying to you. Though I may have awoken your wrath, I never dreamed you would react like you did, giving me a lecture in discipline I didn't deserve. That episode fundamentally altered my perception of you.

I still wish you hadn't left me at a very young age. I miss many things, mostly the father-daughter love – I've been missing that, and still do at this very moment. How I wish you were here with me so that I could experience that sense of love.

Why did you have to beat me while I was naked? I can't recall my age at the time, but I was already a teenager. Don't you think it was unfair for you to do this to your daughter? At least, you could have let me put on some clothes before the beatings began. What kind of a father does such a thing?

And why were you occasionally abusing my mum, your wife? What is wrong with you? That was very unfair of you as well. I would like to know why you behaved like that. My mother didn't deserve an abusive marriage, and it was shameful of you to expose me to that. Like, give me any valid reasons to explain why you decided to do all these things and go rogue! Sorry to say this, but the picture I have of you shows a very ambitious, controlling and self-centered man.

Oh my god! I don't know why I sometimes think of you when Father's Day comes around. I guess you're still my father, even after all you did. Just to let you know, I rarely think of you on that day, it basically depends on my mood.

When you were still in my life, we used to like the same Tanzanian artist, Ali Kiba. We could listen to his albums together. I don't know if you have changed your taste in music, since it's been quite some time since we saw each other.

Hey Dad, before I sign off, I would like you to know something: I hold no grudge. I used to love you, but the love faded away. I do acknowledge your good side, and that you could be a kind and outgoing person; I'll be proud to say that of you.

In case this letter gets to find you, I bet you'll be surprised about how I thought of you this whole time.

    – Your child

CHAPTER 11

by Alex Matiko

Dear Dad,

I'm writing to you keeping in mind that you're no more, may your soul continue resting in peace! An opportunity to share our story presented itself, and I didn't want to miss out on that.

I miss you, and sometimes find myself deep in thought about our times together and the many things we might have done if only you could have lived on.

I miss our greetings. I remember how we used to great each other, referring to ourselves as 'bros.' How about once again saying, "Hello, Brother"? I hope the second universe is good and treating you well. All is well down here, just doing my best. I value the bond we used to have.

I won't fail to remind you about the day when I secretly found you dancing to a Tony Nyadundo jam. Amused, I enjoyed watching you get carried away by the music. Let me tell you, you do have some good moves, bro!

Actually, your appearance at some key events of my life made me proud of you, Honestly, I was excited when you came to my graduation; you being there to witness my academic achievement really meant something.

One day, we woke up early for the farm – just the two of us – without even checking our watches. When we got there, we realized it was only 3 a.m. With nothing else to do, we found a rock to sleep under and waited until 6 a.m., when the sky was finally light enough to see. I'm glad I got to share that experience with you.

Dad, I really wish we could spend more time together, like a father and son should. But with you gone forever, that's just not possible. It's something I still long for, and it hurts knowing I'll never get to experience that for the rest of my life.

I want to thank you for everything you did for me during your time on Earth. Your support for my education meant the world to me – I wouldn't be where I am today if it weren't for you making that choice. Even in your death, I still feel like I owe you, and I appreciate everything you did.

A big thumbs up for raising me in the church. It's helped me discern right from wrong, and instilled good virtues that I continue to live by.

Thank you for being so approachable, which made it easy for me to be close to you and feel fond of you without experiencing any fear. That really strengthened our bond, and the moments we shared were a result of that connection.

You were the most selfless person I've ever known. Throughout our time together, I never felt you were unfair – not even once.

You were such a great soccer fan, and I remember you were also a good player – always playing number 5. Whenever the World Cup comes around, I can't help but think of you and how much I miss you, especially those times when we would bet on the games together.

It's funny, Dad: despite the broad mutual connection and understanding we had, we didn't share any common interests at all. It's strange when I think about it, but it never mattered to us.

As your anniversary approaches, I'd love to celebrate you by sitting down with your brothers, my uncles, and reminiscing about you. Just talking about you will make me so happy.

Dad, I wish I had told you this when I had the chance: I'm sorry. I had no idea you were in an abusive marriage. I know you tried to keep it hidden, staying low-key, but it's heartbreaking that I only learned about it after you were already gone.

I'm grateful that I was able to pick up a few lessons from you while you were still alive. I've learned from you that:

– Staying silent during arguments in marriage can be wise – it helps to prevent further confrontation;

– Having a firm decision-making ability is crucial;

– Being prayerful makes a big difference;

– Having friends is essential because no one can go through life alone.

Father, you were many things – a truly unique person. You were incredibly silent, and some people saw that as being unfriendly, but you were actually very outspoken with friends and even strangers. As God's servant, you never allowed any negative energy in your home. It always surprised me that while you didn't like politicians, you cherished politics.

If this letter ever reaches you in the afterlife, I can picture you reading it with a bright smile.

– *Your son, a.k.a. Bro*

CHAPTER 12

by Nicholas Matthews

Hello Dad,

How are you, and how do you do? Hopefully, this message finds you well. I respectfully send you my greetings. I am glad to report that I'm doing fine.

Whenever I think of the happiest moments I have had with you in my life, I usually remember when I purchased my first car. You were very proud and happy for me on reaching such a milestone. You then encouraged me to keep working hard and aim higher in life.

The day I brought Mum and you to Maasai Mara, I was very excited and delighted. It was an adventure, such a memorable day, and I'm grateful to have shared that with you. We had lots of fun, and the smiles on your faces said it all.

When you showed up for my son's birthday, I was so happy to have you there. Your presence on that special day reminded me of when I was his age, and how you were always there for me at such events. I'm grateful for the time you spent with your grandson that day; the bond you shared was truly special.

I also want to acknowledge that we're all imperfect. I'm sorry for the argument we had; I'd rather not go into details, but I really didn't like how things went. I'm glad I took the time to cool down and gave you the benefit of the doubt. If we had continued the confrontation, it would have only gotten worse and more disrespectful.

The good thing is that we eventually found time to talk and settle our differences in a more civilized way. Sometimes, I wish I had just stayed silent instead of arguing with you on that day.

Growing up, you were always busy, working hard to make ends meet for our family. I really appreciate that. I sometimes wish we had more time to bond and have fun together. I would have cherished that deeply.

Now, it's too late for us to share those moments. I'm the busy one now, working hard to provide a better future for my family, just as you did. Meanwhile, you're retired in the village.

I will always be grateful for the moral guidance, financial support, and mental encouragement you provided. You were my full-time advisor, and you never stopped offering me endless positive advice.

There was a time when I felt your actions were a bit off, and I felt I was being treated unfairly. What really broke my heart was when you said, "I hate you." Those words still confuse me, and I don't fully understand what led to that moment. Despite this, I think I've made peace with it now.

Sometimes, when I think back to President Barack Obama's inauguration, I remember how proud everyone was, and it makes me wish I could make you feel just as proud.

Living life with you has been the best experience I could ask for. Teaching me to drive at a young age sparked my love for cars, and it showed me that we shared an interest in automobiles, which I truly enjoy.

Dad, I want to celebrate you as the best father. Even if I

had a second chance at life, I would still choose you to be my dad.

As long as you're living under this sun, know that I love you, Dad. Even though it might feel a bit strange to say those three words, and I never said them to you in person, I wanted to express it through this letter.

You've been a good father, and I've learned so much from you. You taught me to be hard-working, consistent, and focused. You showed me the importance of being respectful, giving people a second chance, always being punctual, and avoiding situations that might lead to conflict. I'm truly grateful for these life lessons. Thank you.

You're a loving, kind-hearted, dutiful, hardworking, and caring father.

I believe that if this letter gets to you, you will be very proud of yourself and – hopefully – the man you raised me to be.

Bye for now,
- *Your loving son*

CHAPTER 13

by Collins Agesa

Dear Dad,

"Hello, hopefully, you're well." My greeting may sound a bit casual, but that's how I would have relayed it in a personal meeting because I feel you haven't played your role as a father figure in my life. I also think you would be okay with it, because I haven't seen you come to your senses enough to explain why you haven't been there for me.

In my life, there is nothing much I ever had with you. No happiest moments, not even an argument. I wonder! How I wish I would at least have tried and create a bond with you. Whatever happened to us in this life really had a bad impact on you.

I wish to experience fatherly love, but that seems impossible at this stage and moment of life.

I don't even remember you ever doing anything good for me. What I *do* remember is you just punishing me at times, simply because I was delayed coming home from the shop – seriously!

The ups and downs of life – or rather, the struggles of this world – remind me of you. Imagine me going through tough times in life alone, knowing that my father is alive but doesn't give a damn. I'm honestly unsure about how to celebrate you. We missed living life together, and I don't even know if we have any common interests.

I would like to ask you, "Why haven't you been there

for me at all?"

What I have learned from you is that parental love and care are essential to all children in their upbringing. Let there be a more present father figure in any child's life.

You are such a self-centered and uncaring father, and I am sure you wouldn't feel a thing in case this letter were to reach you someday.

– *Your son*

CHAPTER 14

by Winfred Barbari

My dad has been an incredible mentor, and his influence has had a profound and lasting impact upon my life. Although I only saw him on weekends during my childhood, his impact was unmatched.

They say education is the best gift a parent can give a child, and my academic journey is a testament to this. From the start, he believed in me. Even on days when my performance was poor, his faith in my potential never wavered. His encouragement to keep going and work hard has been a cornerstone of my success, helping me reach where I am today.

I am incredibly proud of the consistent support my dad has provided, guiding me every step of the way. Regardless of the challenges and hardships I faced, I always knew I could turn to him. I greatly admire his calm and composed demeanor, as well as his diplomatic and resilient nature. Even when he is clearly upset or angry, he handles the situation with such grace and poise that it never fails to amaze me.

CHAPTER 15

by Teresa Yego

Family was everything to me as a child, but growing up I realized that the family is complete as long as there is love. Before coming to terms with these things, I had to learn and unlearn through observation of what was happening around me.

At Sunday school, they always taught us that a family is made up of a mother, a father, and their children. Even today, we uphold the family of Mary, Jesus, and Joseph as a symbol of "the right" family structure for us Christians, yet a family is more than what is depicted by society.

Dear Father,

There is no informal form of reference for you in my diction. Not that I have run dry of words, but you are like that visitor who only comes home once in a while, for a brief stay. However, you are not the visitor everyone loves, since we all run to hide once we hear your drunken voice outside.

I have seen you around since I was a toddler, but have never really known you. Sadly, I can confidently say that I have known you for years barely half my age. Coming home drunk and late at night was not the problem; you were always shouting and hauling insults at our neighbors, which was rude and inappropriate, yet you were never apologetic – not verbally, not by body language, least of all by expression.

There were good days when you would cook for us and treat us to some nice food, but that was more of a seasonal thing. Your nature was ever-changing like that of a drug addict, happy by day, withdrawn the next minute, or just drunk, your violence only resurfacing when asked for something.

I remember that when I was eight, we were home for the April holidays, which were usually short, and Mum was away for her studies. I asked you for Kiwi shoe polish, and you grabbed me by the thin skin around my then small stomach, on both sides, and held me up in the air. It was painful, and judged by the rage in your eyes, you wanted to throw me against the wall or a hard surface, were it not for the neighbor lady who challenged you to a fight. My brother became your first victim; I bet he does not think of that day as often as I do.

When we moved to our place, things looked better. You started being nicer, but only for a while – when you were still high, I guess. Once everything wore off, you would come home to us, but not in a loving way. You were always shouting and daring to raise your hands at us. Is it because of the stress, Father?

Do you remember when you would verbally reject us, and say we were not yours? Do you remember when you never came to visit me at the hospital, especially in high school when I had pneumonia? You only came on the day I was admitted, and never showed up again. It did not end there. When I was sick or had been admitted to the hospital, you never even called to ask how I was doing. Mum was also in the hospital, and you barely went there. And the blow that made me stop trying was when you left the hospital after I had been referred to a psychiatric clinic.

I can still hear you say to my brother that he'd die. You said it to him when he came home and was very sick, emaciated, and with barely any frame. All you could say was *"utakufa"* ("you'll die"). You kept saying the same thing to my mother, too, time and again as though you were immortal or some god of your own making.

There are not so many joyful days mentioned in this letter. Actually, I can count the number of times everyone was genuinely happy without you ruining it, like you did even on my sister's wedding day. How could you be that selfish? I used to read books and watch series and stories where the father is the best man for her daughter, but you could not even manage to be a good man. It is a shame that my younger sister needs to tell people that she has no father because you bullied her. You showed her that she is worthless, locking her outside the house at 10 in the evening, so dark and very cold. She was barely four years old, and had just been discharged from the hospital a few months prior.

Only my young brother could stand up to you then, and you hated him for that. On that day you told us all, *"Endeni kwa mababa zenu"* ("Go to your fathers") and *"Mwende kwa kina mama yenu"* ("Go to your maternal home"). Well, at least that place always felt like home when my grandfather was there.

I can set aside other experiences because they are just too painful to revisit, and you know that, given what you were doing. As a child, I didn't fully understand what was happening; I was just trying to make sense of it all. As a teenager, I began to grasp the situation more clearly and longed for a good father figure in my life.

I know you were hurt as a child, too – stories we've heard make that clear. You carried that pain, hurt, and trauma with you, and it affected how you treated us. Back then, the norms in your society didn't allow men to confide in others or seek therapy, even though it could have helped. Now, as those norms slowly change, and as you grow older, I realize that the burden you carried was immense. But you projected that pain onto us, and we felt it deeply.

All I can say is that I hope you find peace in your heart and quench the chaos in your mind, so that when God chooses you as our father again, it will be better. We shall all figure it out as a family. Because I want, wish, and yearn for a father, and so do my brothers and sisters.

CHAPTER 16

by Bella Doozy

Daddy Dearest,

I hope this message finds you in good health. While I grew up, we never really had a heart-to-heart conversation to share what was truly going on in our lives. There are many things I'd like to express to you.

First and foremost, I want to express my deepest gratitude. Looking back, I can see the countless ways you have supported and shaped me into who I am today. You have provided for all of my basic needs. Despite being absent during most of my teen years and young adult life, you worked hard to ensure that I had clothes on my back, food on the table, and was able to attend the best school available in our area. You allowed me to spread my wings, fly, express myself, and pursue my passion. You have always been there to give me the advice I needed to make good life decisions.

Lately, I've been reflecting on the moments we shared and the lessons I learned. During my childhood, I grew accustomed to having a father who was often absent. It didn't bother me much at first, but it gradually created a distance between us. As I grew up, I felt a lack of connection with you. We hardly spoke, and I don't recall you asking about anything other than the basics such as my grades, behavior in school, and school fees.

You always pushed my siblings and me to be nothing

but the best. You instilled in me the importance of hard work, which has become an integral part of my life. Now, all I strive for is to be the best. I am a go-getter, and that quality comes from you. It's one of my prime attributes and a gift I carry with me every day.

I've always strived to be the best, with the goal of earning your approval. This ambition continues to drive me to this day. My journey isn't just for my own benefit; it's also to make you proud as a father.

My life has been like the sea: calm at times, waves crashing against the rocks at others times. I felt elated when you praised my primary school grades. However, I still recall receiving a message about my KCSE exam results and feeling disappointed in myself. Even more daunting was the fear of your reaction. I phoned you, and I'll never forget how deeply disheartened you sounded. Your disappointment shattered me, and I felt like a failure for not receiving the approval I so desperately sought from my father. I remember breaking down for hours, and Mom spent the day encouraging and comforting me because she understood how hearing your disappointment had affected me.

When I advanced to the next level, I made a promise to work twice as hard to regain your approval. I couldn't start where I wanted with my grades, so I had to take a different path. However, one moment that will always stay with me is when you sat me down and told me that I should pursue my passion, without any pressure to do anything else. Your words filled me with hope and empowerment. It meant so much to me when you said that you would support me until I could stand on my own. It was exactly what I needed to hear, especially from my father.

Because of that, I felt the need to repay you by never disappointing you again. I stayed true to my word, and became the best student in my class, earning a distinction. This was a proud achievement for me, especially because I could feel your approval.

Our relationship wasn't easy as I grew up. We didn't see eye to eye most days, and I often felt frustrated, as though I had to work twice as hard to meet your expectations. Among your children, I was the one who needed extra effort on your part to ensure that my school needs were met. There was a period of about six months when I refused to speak to you directly, choosing instead to communicate through Mom. As a teenager, I was quite confrontational, and it seemed like every conversation we had ended in an argument.

I know I didn't make things easy for you. I was always on your case about something different every day. It took you six months to realize that your firstborn daughter wasn't speaking to you. However, I'm glad that once you noticed, you took the initiative to ask about it. I was thankful that we were able to resolve that issue and put it behind us.

I always wanted to be close to you, but the more I tried, the harder it seemed to connect. Eventually, I stopped trying. You would come home for a weekend, we would exchange a few pleasant words, and that would be the end of it. While you were away, it felt like you were just a memory in my mind. I felt envious of the connection you had with my younger sister. The two of you seemed naturally close; your relationship flowed effortlessly. I wanted the same for me. My sister is one of the smartest and kindest people I have ever met. She made you proud from the start, and I could see it in the way you two talked and interacted.

My personal life became challenging to the point where I found it difficult to balance my life and maintain good relations with you, Mom, and my siblings. I ended up becoming distant to all of you. Thankfully, with God's help, I was able to break free from that struggle and get back on track. It took time, but when you came back home, we were able to bond and build a relationship stronger than ever before. I'm grateful, as an adult, that I can depend upon and talk to you effortlessly.

Dad, you are the best man I have ever met and my first love. You are resilient, hardworking, a provider, a protector, and a good listener. You give great life advice. I love that you don't lie or sugarcoat reality; you tell it as it is because honesty is the best policy. Just from having you, I know what qualities to expect in the person I want to spend my life with.

Losing a job can be a burden, especially for parents with school-aged children. It has been heartening to see how this setback has drawn us closer as a family. I cherish every day when we can call or text each other for a casual chat, and – most importantly – when we can have dinner together, sharing our individual experiences at the place we have called home for the past 12 years.

I am truly happy to have you as my father. Given a chance to choose again, I would still choose you, Daddy dearest.

With lots of love,

– *Your firstborn daughter*

CHAPTER 17

by Fratello Gemello

I and my four older siblings were being raised by our single mother when life became very challenging. At the age of six, I was enrolled into a different school, and subsequently moved to a superior school for my primary education.

At that time, Mom was married to a man who took very good care of us. However, another man – in his late thirties – often brought us shopping, yet we barely knew him. My mother was tight-lipped about revealing secrets, so we never inquired.

In 2008, as I prepared to sit for my final exams, this same man attended my rehearsals. I couldn't explain his reasons for being there, but it did not impact me. As I took my KCPE examinations, nothing distracted me, and I performed well when the results were announced.

In 2009, I enrolled into a high school for my secondary education. I often visited my elder sister, who resided in a small town. Frequently, I encountered the same man who used to bring us shopping, always wearing a broad smile, yet I still had no clue about his identity. Upon inquiring, I learned that he was employed at a nearby institution. Not knowing much about him, I didn't dwell on it and life went on as normal.

One day, during my holidays, I decided to visit my uncle, who lived about two kilometers away from the institution. While there, I had a conversation with my aunt, who disclosed some shocking secrets about my true identity. I was so overwhelmed that I felt my energy drain away. She started by explaining that I had been kept in the dark all this time because my mother had wished for it to be so. She went on to reveal that the man I had always known as my father was not my biological father, and that my mother had been expelled from her home after it was discovered that I was not a member of that family.

The ordeal began around two years before I was born. My mother went to visit her aunt, and ended up staying for nearly a year. Upon her return, she was pregnant, with the delivery date fast approaching. Her husband refused to accept the pregnancy, and consequently chased her away. She found refuge in her father's home. Overwhelmed, she nearly took her life, but my aunt supported her through everything until she gave birth.

Following this brief disclosure, my mother assured me that the truth would emerge one day, and I would learn the identity of my father. I often felt the urge to confront her for answers, but was too young to do so.

My ordinary level education passed by swiftly. I joined the advanced level for two years, but resorted to various hustles due to a lack of funds for university. Life's hardships led me to travel to a neighboring country in search of better opportunities. Shortly after arriving, I received a call from my sister informing me that the man who used to bring us shopping had passed away. I was devastated but powerless to change the situation. After three years in the city, I felt it was enough and made the decision to return home.

Back there, some people came looking for me, claiming that I was part of their family; something I did not understand. They said that the deceased man was indeed my father, and that he had left clear instructions for to them to go looking for me. They even claimed to know my mother very well. From their description of my mother, they surely knew everything about her, even some details that were unbeknownst to me. I was surprised to learn that everyone at home almost knew the entire story but kept me in the dark. I asked why, and was told that my mother had instructed them not to disclose anything to anyone.

Alas, I came to know my real father when he was no more, and so I have not experienced any fatherly love throughout my life.

After the whole drama, I was finally incorporated into the family. I was overjoyed to meet my brothers and sisters, uncles and aunts, and everyone else. After some time, a ceremony was held, and all of us were brought together for a special meal and family union.

Today, we live happily as children of the same man regardless of our mothers. I'm very happy about that, and also happy for everyone who worked tirelessly to ensure that long-ignored needs and wishes have been fulfilled.

I don't know whether what happened was inevitable, but I am sure that God was behind everything. Let my father continue resting in peace!

CHAPTER 18

by Jombaa Onkel

As the saying goes, anyone can be a father, but it takes someone special to be a dad. My father, I must concede, was just that and nothing more. Our relationship was sporadic at best, almost nonexistent. When I was three or four years old, I became aware of a man who spent some time at our house. He was never quite present, but I would see him once in a while, just like a bigger version of myself. I didn't really comprehend who this person was.

My father was previously married with a family of his own. My mother was widowed at an early age, and her matrimonial family sent her back to live with her mother. My maternal grandmother was a single parent of nine who raised her kids single-handedly after breaking up with her husband. I never got the chance to meet my grandfather, but do recall my aunt saying that her father had passed away and been buried without her knowledge.

My mother had three kids from her previous marriage, two sons and one daughter. My grandmother once told me that after the girl was born, the father had been killed over a family dispute.

Upon arrival, my mother had been very upset and not in her right mind. She was strong-willed and not easily influenced by others, would generally follow her mind. She was supposedly the "best" among her siblings, the one with the cleanest heart and the purest intentions.

After settling in, my mother decided that it was time to start over and build a new life. She had her in-laws take custody of her children, and went back to dating. My mother was reportedly the prettiest woman to ever exist in that area. Going out and socializing led to her meeting my father, by then a married man, which eventually brought me and my two younger brothers into existence.

Growing up, it was pretty much us three siblings taking care of ourselves. My father was not present, so in case I got to look at a picture, I couldn't recognize his face and point out that this was him. My mother wasn't much around either.

One night when I was around five years old, my parents argued fiercely. I couldn't understand what was going on, but saw the rage and anger on their faces all night long.

We used to live in Eldoret town. One day, my father left for work early in the morning, while we were still asleep. Later that morning, around 10:00 or 11:00 am, my mother dressed us in matching outfits – white shirts and black trousers – which made us look like twins. She then took us to visit our father at his workplace. When we arrived, we waited in the reception area while my mother went into his office.

My father was a banker, and had a nice office with a glass door. From the reception area, I could see my parents inside, arguing – they were throwing their hands in the air, but it wasn't a fight. The argument went on for quite some time, during which the receptionist brought us some orange soda. I remember holding my younger brother while the other sat beside me as we drank. Then suddenly, my mother stormed out of the office in tears, and left the building. My father didn't come out, but the receptionist soon approached us. She told us to leave the office and walk out of the premises to the gate. I wasn't sure if that was exactly what my father had instructed her to say, but that's what we did.

We brought with us the same small blue bag we had carried that morning, and ended up sitting on it outside the gate. We were just kids, too young to understand what was happening, but were left sitting there in the scorching sun from noon until six in the evening. Around that time, our father's car drove by. I remember feeling excited, thinking he had come to pick us up because it was our special day to visit him at work. But to my surprise, he simply drove off. That was the last time I saw him.

That was the last memory I have of my father, and it's the saddest one. We've never talked about it as a family, and maybe doing so would help us heal, but it's caused some pain I'm still working through. I'm still on a journey of healing. The thought that he could leave his own children on the streets and just drive off is painful and traumatizing. The wound runs deep, it's incredibly sad.

While outside the gate, an in-law of my mum's twin sister recognized us as the town kids who spoke Swahili. He asked us what we were doing there, to which we responded that we had no place to go. He decided to take us to my aunt's place. She, in turn, brought us to our grandmother, who took us in, saying, "Okay, let me raise these kids, that is all I can do."

We didn't get to see our mother for a while. Some

people say it took her two weeks to return, but to me it felt like forever. Everything was changing very quickly, so that we didn't know what to do or how to pick ourselves up.

Staying at our grandmother's place, we began to experience a different way of life. Everything felt unique and unfamiliar. Anyone who has spent time at their African grandmother's house will probably agree that it feels very different from their own home.

The house was smaller than what we were used to. Adapting to this new environment presented other challenges, such as a language barrier. I struggled to communicate with my grandmother about certain things, and my brother couldn't eat certain meals because they were too unfamiliar. *These kids don't understand how things work here*, my grandmother seemed to be thinking. The situation became even more amusing once the neighbors realized that we were from the town and spoke only Kiswahili.

Neighbors were thrilled to be sending their kids to my grandmother's place to play with us. We would teach them Kiswahili, and they would teach us our mother's native language. As a result, we ended up learning our mother tongue. We even wound up teaching our uncles Kiswahili, which they speak fluently today. In return, they taught us how to improve in our mother tongue, which I now speak fluently.

My mother returned drunk. I had seen my parents drunk before, but this time felt different. Our once stable life lay in ruins, and our reality was harsh. As Mum stepped inside, everyone stared at her, and even I looked at her as if she were a stranger.

When she spoke about my father, I wasn't entirely sure if what she said was true. Yet, I had a strong sense that he had passed away. It was clear that things were falling apart, and I knew I had to be sharp, sensitive and careful, especially with my younger siblings depending on me. Unsure of who else would take care of us, I ended up raising my brothers for quite some time.

We were left without a father or any male figure. With just my grandmother and our often-drunk mother to take care of us, our lives became filled with uncertainty. In fact, my mother's alcoholism led to her being absent for extended periods of time.

My aunt, whom I deeply respect and who played a significant role in raising and caring for us, eventually noticed that my mother wasn't paying attention to our education. When I was about six or seven years old, my aunt took me away from her.

My mother often went out, drank excessively, and spent little time at home, returning only once or twice a month. As time went on, she became increasingly absent from our lives due to worsening difficulties. I eventually came to understand that she was suffering from depression, though it went unrecognized by everyone around us. I wish I had been old enough to support and comfort her, as even her own siblings dismissed her as merely troublesome and insane.

My aunt was already dealing with her own challenges, including a husband battling alcoholism, but she took me in to help my mother. She tried to provide stability for us, but life remained very difficult.

Later, my mother became pregnant again and had my younger brother. His paternity remains unknown, which I find deeply saddening. For years, I kept this fact hidden, but now I openly acknowledge him as my brother despite the mystery surrounding his father. Although we have different fathers, he remains my brother, and that connection is important to me.

I remember the details of my mother's pregnancy vividly. One afternoon, around 3:00 PM, she came back home and went to a tree in the plantation near our house. My brothers and I were alone at home. There, she gave birth to our younger brother. Afterward, she asked me to go and call her twin sister. Her sister arrived and helped her with the delivery. Thankfully, my brother was okay.

After three days, my mother left me alone with the newborn. This is the saddest part of my story. I was only a child myself, and didn't know how to care for a baby who was just three days old. My mother had simply woken up one morning and left, so I had to manage on my own. To help my brother, I would give him my finger to suckle, hoping he would think it was breast milk. I also boiled some water to give him.

During this time, my grandmother was away visiting her brother and was gone for two to three days at a time. When she returned, she found that we had borrowed milk from some neighbors. I had tried to boil the milk for the baby, but it went bad before I could use it. Seeing the spoiled milk, my grandmother told me not to give it to the baby. I didn't know how to handle the situation, and can't remember how life continued.

At the time when my aunt wanted me to move to her place so I could start school, I had been open to the idea. The trauma and challenges I had faced made me eager to leave, though I felt held back by the sense of responsibility for my brothers. I spent a few days with my mother, contemplating how to leave. She was quite strict and often seemed to see my father in me, perhaps because I resemble him closely in appearance, if not in character.

While my mother and the baby were asleep, I walked to my aunt's place, which wasn't far away. The next day, my aunt took me to a nearby primary school to see if they would enroll me. It was either the second or third term of the school year, and I began attending school towards the end of the term.

My mother continued struggling with alcoholism, and I often found myself carrying my younger sibling on my back while my mother hurled insults at my aunt, accusing her of favoring me because I was smarter than her own children. My aunt never took offense, understanding that her sister was grappling with significant issues.

I spent most of my early years being raised by my aunt. As I continued my education, my uncle, whom I affectionately called Dad, took on the paternal role in my life. Despite his alcoholism and the disruptions it caused when he was intoxicated, he was a calm and supportive presence when sober. There were nights when he would cast us out and lock the door behind him, choosing to sleep alone. By then, I had come to terms with life's complexities and learned to adapt.

When I started at a nearby primary school, a typical old public institution, it was common to see students barefoot or without proper uniforms, as these were acquired gradually. At the nursery level, my height and apparent intelligence led my aunt to suggest skipping the baby class and joining the top class to see if I could handle it. If not, I would repeat the year. A month later, during the end-term exams, I surprised everyone by ranking second in the class. The top student was my best friend. My disappointment wasn't rooted in resentment but in my drive to excel.

When I didn't win, I returned home and cried to my aunt. To my surprise, she told me, "You've done very well," even though I had been outperformed by another student. Her viewpoint was hard for me to grasp at the time. She noticed my silent demeanor, a change that stemmed from my trauma, and realized she needed to step in further to help.

As the next term began, I started to truly understand what having a father meant. When I started Class One, my aunt made an effort to make me feel comfortable, and my uncle aimed to reassure me by taking on a father role. He promised to take care of me, saying that I would learn to do things that boys and men do. It was a learning process, as I was unfamiliar with the different roles boys and girls had.

As the eldest child, I was both a child and a caretaker for my siblings. I knew how to handle household chores like washing dishes, collecting firewood, and sweeping. I even began learning to cook. Although my grandmother didn't have cattle, we did have sheep. My younger brother was responsible for the sheep, while I took on other tasks.

As a young boy, I often felt lost and confused, especially since my cousins were older and I was the youngest. In first grade, my uncle – who was also my cousin's dad – expressed a desire for me to work alongside him. He promised to teach me everything, starting with planting trees even in the rain, which I found quite enjoyable. We also worked on fencing, and it was amusing how he had me hold the nails while he hammered them. He was the one who introduced me to these tasks and guided me through them.

My uncle entrusted me with the responsibility of caring for the cattle, ensuring they had water every day, and taking care of the sheep by feeding them and providing water.

During that time, I didn't have to fetch water myself; instead, my uncle would wake up early to fill the metal drums. This way, when I led the cattle out of their shelter, they could drink from the drums or we would take them to the river after grazing. We often swam in the river while the cattle quenched their thirst and frolicked in the mud. We took great pleasure in watching the cows playfully spar. These are cherished memories from my childhood, and I attribute them all to my uncle.

While I was excelling at my school, my aunt and uncle decided, "This boy is performing exceptionally well, so let's move him to a better school where he can face some competition." I was transferred, but eventually my aunt and family could no longer afford the nominal fee required. We used to bring maize and beans to school as a form of payment.

My uncle suggested to my aunt, "You know, there are

scholarships available for bright students. Why don't we apply for them?" So they did, and I was fortunate to receive a scholarship that covered a portion of my school fees and also provided me with a complete school uniform for an entire year.

In 2007, my life's trajectory changed when my grandmother fell ill. Reflecting, I lost my mother when I was in first grade. My mother's twin sister took in the youngest sibling, while the other two of us stayed with our grandmother. We attended the same school, each of us a class apart. The youngest was fully adopted by my aunt, and is regarded as her child to this day.

When my grandmother fell ill, I returned to her home to begin caring for both her and my brother. I was in fourth grade at the time. Without a father or any support, I once again found myself in a situation where I had to manage everything on my own.

While caring for my grandmother, we had one uncle who was often inebriated and another who lived just across the fence. I'm not sure if they had a falling out with their mother, but the uncle from across the fence never came to greet her, even when she was ill, which left me puzzled.

On December 31, 2008, I spent the entire night conversing with my grandmother while she was in severe pain. In the middle of the night, she began to vomit substances that resembled minced meat, which was frightening. Throughout the night, she shared how our father had abandoned us and her ignorance of his whereabouts.

"You three arrived, and I was unaware of your mother's

whereabouts, who she was involved with, but she had tales about this person. There's no legal or formal confirmation of their marriage, only stories of this man's visit."

She shared these stories with me, including how much we would suffer without a father, lacking not only a paternal figure but also an identity, uncertain of where we belonged. She expressed doubts about her sons caring for us as their nephews, describing them as unkind and indifferent. This was her narrative throughout the night.

"You must now rise to the occasion. Though not old enough to care for your siblings, it falls upon you. There's nothing to be done, no inheritance from me, and it seems I won't be here much longer to provide care. Wherever you go, I pray that God will be with you. May God's presence comfort you in any new family that welcomes you after I depart. Our circumstances are beyond my control."

My grandmother and I spent the whole night weeping. As I cried, my siblings were asleep. When she vomited, I was startled and unsure of what to do, but I knew I couldn't just sit there – I had to go call my uncle. My uncle is central to this narrative; he's why I've grown to resent the men in our family. It led me to realize that men are not inherently good, which made me question why I was born a man amidst all these people.

I rushed to my uncle's house because he was the nearest neighbour. Calling out to him across the fence, it was around 3 AM, and I was only in shorts, no shirt. When I told him our grandmother was ill, vomiting something strange, and begged for his help, he simply said, "It's night, go back to sleep; you're making noise."

Without hesitation, I knew I had to get to my aunt's house quickly. Running through the dense forest, I arrived at her door, pounding and yelling for her to help our grandmother. My aunt immediately sprang into action, wearing her pajamas.

We returned to my grandmother's home. At that point, my aunt took over to help her; it was out of my hands. As dawn broke, I rushed to inform my other aunts that Grandma was ill. They all arrived, and escorted her to the hospital. About 200 meters from the house, my grandmother paused and looked back at us, the three of us watching her leave. She gazed at us for a few seconds, maybe a minute, then continued on her way. I believe that at that moment, she was silently telling us, "I feel for you, the young ones. I'm uncertain about what lies ahead for you, but such is life – it has now begun."

That was the last day we spent with our grandmother at her house. We were left alone, and I assumed the role of a father to my siblings. Acting as both a father and a mother often made me wonder if I would ever become a parent myself. Could I care for my own children, having fulfilled these roles?

Life continued. We managed to survive. We often had to borrow food because we had nothing. I made many sacrifices to ensure our survival, and took care of my siblings to the best of my ability.

Sadly, we lost Grandma in August, and she was laid to rest. During the mourning period, it seemed everyone forgot about the children she had left behind at home.

Two weeks after the burial, my uncle, who couldn't care for himself, would still visit us when we were alone, seeking food and asking, "Have you cooked?" We were soon to be separated; I moved in with my uncle just across the fence, my immediate brother went to stay with my aunt where I had previously lived, and my other brother went to live with our eldest aunt, joining her grandchildren of similar age.

My uncle was expected to assume a fatherly role, but he never fulfilled any role at all. He never showed concern for me, focusing only on his children, ensuring they attended school and that their fees were paid. The experience of having a father figure once again eluded me.

In 2009, while staying at my uncle's place, one of my cousins told me that my dad was looking for me. I was stunned. The idea that my father was searching for me seemed incredible. I couldn't fathom who this person was or what he would be like. It was so shocking that I just went along with the plan to visit him the next day at 3 PM.

That night, I couldn't sleep. I was filled with anxiety and uncertainty about what to expect. How would I face this man? Would he appear monstrous or ordinary? Would he have features similar to mine, like the way he walked or his eyes? The thought of meeting him was overwhelming, and I was consumed with questions and fear about what the encounter would be like.

Where does he live? I thought he was dead – certain he was. Could he be a ghost or something? Such thoughts tormented me throughout the night.

The next day, our cousin led us to what I thought would be our father's place. When we arrived, my cousin asked questions that suggested she was aware of our father's passing, although she didn't seem shocked, which confused me further. I had been in a process of healing, having grown up believing my father was deceased. Just as I was coming to terms with the idea that he might be alive, I was faced with the sudden revelation that he had indeed passed away and had already been buried.

Our stepmother, who knew of our existence, was unwelcoming and seemed intent on rejecting us. She avoided introducing us to others, and quickly tried to usher us away to speak privately, making it clear that she wanted us to leave. I was overwhelmed and confused, struggling to understand what was happening.

Despite the turmoil, we stayed in town because some extended family members advised against returning to our mother's home. We spent the night there, and the following day we were informed of a family meeting. Such gatherings are customary in our culture to discuss arrangements for the deceased and the family's welfare after such a loss.

My stepmother had assumed we had left the day before and not returned. To her surprise, we showed up, and the meeting began. As the proceedings unfolded, the situation became increasingly chaotic, especially when it was time for our introduction. We had taken our seats, and the meeting continued without much pause.

My father's brother, who had also helped raise him and was like a grandfather to me, was there. He tried to speak with my siblings, but the atmosphere was tense. Some were drinking, and the situation grew more complicated. He made an effort to address the family's well-being after their loss, but his attempts were met with rebellion.

Things escalated quickly when my immediate brother began to run away, causing the meeting to be abruptly dismissed as people feared for his safety. I stayed behind with the others, while my cousin ran after my brother to ensure he was safe. Left with my younger sibling, we both started crying, overwhelmed by the turmoil and the stark reality of our situation.

My brother was eventually rescued from afar, but he refused to return home. As a result, we were told to wait by the road for a matatu. While we waited, some relatives offered to drop us in town for our journey back. We shared a meal with our extended family, and then returned to our previous location, feeling utterly disheartened. At that point, I had lost all hope.

In the midst of the confusion and rapid changes, I felt lost as if everything was moving too quickly and unpredictably. Eventually, we all returned to our respective homes and tried to carry on with our lives, each of us grappling with the aftermath in our own way.

Life at my uncle's place wasn't great, but I persevered nonetheless. My cousin, who brought us to our father's family, is a professional teacher. She had been teaching at the same school and working alongside another distant cousin on my father's side.

One day at work, my cousin overheard a colleague recounting tales of his origins. He spoke of his hometown and other personal anecdotes. My cousin recognized a connection and exclaimed, "Oh, you're from there? I have cousins who hail from the same place, but they were left by their father." She went on to share our story, detailing how they had cared for us despite not knowing our father.

This man informed her that our father and his mother were siblings, which left my cousin astonished. Consequently, she invited him to visit us. He accepted because our location was conveniently close to their travel route. Upon arrival, they encountered only me; I was in the kitchen at my uncle's house, attempting to cook, while my siblings played elsewhere. They didn't meet anyone else since I was near the gate. My cousin approached, and I assumed she had come simply to greet me.

My cousin mentioned that this person belonged to our family. At that moment, I was indifferent; I no longer wanted to dwell on it. It was a topic I chose not to focus on because it continued to cause me pain. Then, they departed.

I believe it was around June or July, just a few months after my father passed away in April 2009. Life continued, and we moved past that period. However, my situation at my uncle's worsened, and I had to flee. Before I left, the villagers began to voice their concerns about my well-being. They spoke to my aunt, who had taken in my immediate brother. In response, she sent my brother to speak with me, seeing if I would be willing to move back and stay with them, as she had heard that things were not going well for me.

My brother would come over on the weekends to help

me with some chores. As we worked and talked together, he would mention things like, "You know, auntie wants you to visit," and he would ask about my life, whether I felt like staying here or wanted to move back there. I told him, "OK, let me think about it." Then things got worse. I was denied food, yes, the day before I left, and that's when I made the decision: *You know what? I'm leaving!*

The following day, fueled by anger, I took on the task of tackling the laundry. I washed my clothes, dried them, and ironed them meticulously, as I had resolved to leave. No one knew of my plans to depart that day. As evening approached, I decided not to do anything around the house, because I would end up being blamed regardless of what I did or didn't do.

That evening, I went to the place where I used to sleep – my grandmother's abandoned house. I pretended to go to bed at 10 PM. As a result, everything was left undone: the lunch utensils were unwashed, the cattle were not brought back from grazing, and the paraffin was not purchased. They usually sent me to buy it at night, despite the distance and the dangers, like being chased by dogs and encountering drunkards, all while I was just a young boy.

In my haste to escape, my only thought was to vanish into the forest. As I hurried along, my aunt's words came to me – she had said, "If you ever need to leave, come to my place." So, after spending some time crying in the forest that night, I resolved to go there.

When I visited my aunt's place, things took an unexpected turn. Upon my arrival, she expressed sympathy for my struggles, but then instructed me to leave the next morning at 7 AM. She wanted to avoid the gossip and sensitive stares from those who knew I had come from my uncle's home.

Early the next day, she woke me up and directed me to stay with my cousin, the one who had previously taken us to my father's family. This cousin played a crucial role during that transitional time, and became a key figure in my life.

She brought me to my cousin, who lived in Eldoret at the time. During the holiday, my cousin reached out to a colleague and said, "Remember the boy I mentioned that we visited? He's now staying with me. Could you come over so I can introduce him to you? Then, perhaps you could take him to your hometown to see if he likes it there." The colleague agreed enthusiastically, saying, "Yeah, yeah, yeah, no problem, let's do it."

I agreed because, at that point, I was indifferent to everything. If I found a breakthrough, great; if not, that was fine too – even the thought of dying seemed preferable. With this mindset, I traveled to my late father's distant hometown, accompanied by a stranger who claimed to be from there.

Upon arrival, he introduced me to my father's older brother. Recognizing him from my father's funeral, I felt a sense of relief. Trusting the man who had brought me there, I began to feel more comfortable in the presence of family. During my stay, my uncle shared many stories, and his happiness was evident. He indeed played a significant role in my life during that time.

He spoke to me as if I were his son. I still saw him as a

grandfather, yet he regarded me as his nephew, the son of his brother. He shared tales of siblings who left home and never returned, who no longer remembered their way back.

"Now that you're here, I want you to carry on and uphold your father's legacy."

This man had been sharing all these stories with me, and the father he referred to had passed away before I even got to see him. Yet, now I felt a sense of love and belonging. My uncle revealed his plans for me, for us, for the three of us. I was amazed, pondering upon why he held such deep concern for us. I have this tendency to be open with people; but until I truly get to know someone, I reserve my trust.

"I'm not sure why you're so interested in me," I told him. Especially when someone grows up without love and attention, and then suddenly finds it, it can be confusing to interpret it correctly.

I ended up staying there for about a week, although we had only made plans for three days. After the third day, the cousin who had dropped me off went back to his place, leaving me with nowhere else to go.

The next morning, at my father's place, I was amazed to wake up to the sight of the hills. I arrived during the rainy season when everything was lush and green. The hills, roads, and waterfalls made the place stunningly beautiful. I found myself waking up early each day just to gaze at the hills. Coming from a flatter part of the Rift Valley, the hilly landscape here was a stark contrast. Everything seemed scattered and uneven.

The man arrived and took me back. Meanwhile, my

cousin on the other side had deceived everyone. Whenever someone visited her, she would claim I had gone to town with friends, grandparents, or elsewhere, keeping my whereabouts unknown to my mother's side of the family.

Upon my return, my cousin was visibly relieved, exclaiming, "Whoops, you're back!" The worry was evident, as I had overstayed.

More uncertainty and drifting followed until one individual finally stepped in and assumed full responsibility, declaring, "I will take care of these children." My maternal aunt was overjoyed, thrilled that our family had come together. Then we transitioned from living with our mother to moving in with our father's side of the family.

I moved in with my aunt, who took me in from day one. Her husband filled the paternal role in my life, and my aunt became like a mother to me. He raised me as his own son, and has always been there for me. He noticed that I was different from his biological children, and treated me with special care and understanding.

He listens to me attentively and is sensitive to my concerns, even when they might seem unclear. He understands the void created by the absence of a father figure in my early life and the various changes I've gone through. His presence in my life has been so seamless that I sometimes wonder if my biological father would have been able to step into that role in the same way. I'm not sure.

Sometimes, I sense that God has a grand plan for me. Even when things seemed chaotic, I was certain of a greater design. I found the best father figure in him. Upon us meeting, he began to weave himself into my life. Despite my attempts to resist and pull away, his efforts drew me back. I found myself wanting to spend time with him, eager to see him, to be in his presence, to hear his stories, and to understand him. He listened to me, acknowledged my flaws, and would simply look at me and laugh.

He is a kind man and undoubtedly one of the biggest role models in my life. He has taken great care of me. When I moved and had to transfer to another school in class eight, he would visit me. Despite the distance, he made the effort to come to see me at school, bringing bread, and would visit occasionally, which I fondly recall. His motivation has supported me from class eight to the present. The person I have become is shaped by his guidance and efforts.

I recall my high school days when he inspired me. I was a good performer, not the best, but still among the top students. The competition was fierce in the best school, yet I managed to stay at the top. He took pride in me. Once, I ranked seventh out of five hundred and seventeen students, surpassing five hundred and ten peers. Seeing my report card, Dad remarked, "You've tried," which puzzled me. *What do you mean by 'You've tried'?* I wondered. Then he explained, "In our family, people are exceptionally intelligent. You're one of them, very smart. You should be in the first position."

It took me a while to realize that this man only wanted what was best for me. As a teenager, you're at a point where you want to explore. The environment I entered opened my mind; they were open to me. I was permitted to be myself, and it felt liberating. I felt free to discuss anything with Dad.

During one holiday, my aunt, whom I now call Mom, allowed me to refer to her as such. These two individuals, my mom and her husband, have become my parents. We stayed and lived together.

I discussed my post-school aspirations with my dad. He has taught me how to interact with others, as I've noticed he never argues or has conflicts with anyone. His guidance has truly shaped me. During my time on campus, he was a constant source of advice, sharing the do's and don'ts. Campus life can be wild, but his support was unwavering. I owe him immensely; for all that I am and all my current reasoning, I consider his perspective – what he would think or advise. He always has my best interests at heart, as well as everyone else's. He desires to see me succeed and prays for me. His genuine love is evident, and whenever I'm troubled, I take solace in knowing I have a father to turn to at home.

At this stage of my life, as I'm transitioning and trying to settle, he has been the pivotal person I confide in. I share updates with him and seek his counsel on my plans, and he guides me – advising what to do and what not to do. We collaborate on ideas; he's been my confidant, a father figure, and so much more to me. In this regard, I would credit him with more than a thousand percent. This isn't to diminish the contributions of others who have been there for me – they've all done their utmost.

However, when it comes to my biological father, we never shared a life or any meaningful interaction. I've always seen him merely as a sperm donor who departed. That's the extent of the story I can tell about my dad.

ABOUT THE AUTHORS

Erick Ochieng Otieno is a Kenyan poet and author, who has left an indelible mark on the literary world. His impactful contributions include being featured in the "Wings of My Dreams" Anthology, a prestigious collection compiled by Shupta Gupta, where two of his poems are showcased.

Vivienne Kapkarich is a Kenyan poet and author. "Eminent Desire," her collection of over 80 emotional poems, is published by Novelty Fiction. Her work has been featured in anthologies such as "The Unspoken Chronicles," "Writing Woman Anthology," and "The Wings of My Dreams."

Printed in Great Britain
by Amazon